SHE MADE WAVES

To Live a Life of Delight through Desire

Kiki Carr

SHE MADE WAVES: To live a life of delight through desire

For information contact:
www.kikicarr.com

Book and Cover design by Sylvie Leveiller

ISBN:

Hardcover: 978-1-7771760-1-3
Paperback: 978-1-7771760-3-7
Ebook: 978-1-7771760-2-0
Kindle: 978-1-7771760-4-4

First Edition: January 2021

BALMORAL
PRESS

CONTENTS

to you, the reader, the reason in its birth

INTRODUCTION

Writing is an expression.
Reading is an experience.

I'VE LEARNED OVER that last few years, that if I want to change things around me, I must first change them in myself. But how could I do that, and where would I start? I was intrigued by this idea of living a happy life - a life of delight. I have created a roadmap for myself through research, reading books, attending workshops, classes, trips, and conferences. This roadmap is what I use to get back on track, should the train ever derail itself (I, being the train of course). The concept is simple in theory: To live a life of delight, I must first pinpoint what I desire and then go after it. But sometimes I have lessons to learn along the way, things to accept through the journey, and other things to let go of. There is humility in accepting that my current situation is my current choice - whether good or bad. When I can accept and move toward setting practices in place, I can allow myself to evolve toward my desire.

This book is a journey through mindfulness wonder, accepting what is, self reflection, letting go of what no longer serves me, understanding by being, and learning lessons for change.

I designed this book with the chapters in a particular sequence, because this is the journey I take to move toward my desires to live a life of delight. You can enjoy this process from start to finish, or skip to the section that most speaks to you. Use this as part of your daily mindful practice and flip through, or use as journal prompts.

Water has been a very important part of this experience. I learn from its movements, I feel connected while bathing in it, and I listen to its mindful way of existence. This connection has driven me to seek out bodies of water and take in what it has to offer. You'll see photos throughout this book, which are just a glimpse of the spaces that hold important stories for me.

I wrote these words as a documented self reflection and creative expression. You are now holding it as a way to experience something new. When I serve myself in my daily practice, I open the door to wander in delight. Through this, I create ripples that turn into waves.

Spend this time for yourself, because I sure did while writing it.

And so it begins...

ACCEPTANCE

When you can accept what is, you can move forward without.

Moving toward the life I want doesn't take courage, it takes desire.

The pushing and pulling
Like waves on sand

For surfer's delight
To glide above

Some float along
Others may sink

But which is right
Or which is wrong

There is no answer
Just strength in knowing

Which one you are
And which way you're going.

Can we love the simplicity
In the dance of the wind
The fire's song
And the water's writing?

In their arms
I am the child
Earth's pride and joy.

For if Kingdoms crash
And systems fall
She'll still be here
To embrace my all.

I am holding
Myself accountable
For how I interpret
Your words.

It is not you
To whom I seek
But my own strife
In what I need.

I am my keeper
I do not need

To follow their words
When all they lead

Is an unkept trail
With needles and thorns

And I always had
A compass at hand.

I cannot change it
I *can* change me.

I cannot force
The butterfly's cocoon
But I can learn
From its transition.

Lost in the dark
And my way out
Is searching for slivers
To guide me through.

Stormy weather
Brings tides of change

To clear the depths
Of hidden debris

And unearth pollution
Surrendered to shore.

And what are we
If not the sums
The good and bad
Our deepest truth.
Should I regret
Or thank them well
For I am not
Myself without.

There is much to change
Or none at all
The trick is finding
In which you fall.

Held back
By my need
To seek and analyze.

Allowing
Brought the ease
With acceptance at the helm.

I saunter forward
With a smile
For joy is found in me.

LESSONS

It's in the learning that we stop repeating.

We are not meant to stay the same,
so why do we condemn ourselves while we learn?

I wonder what will happen
Once I figure out

How to break the dam
That's holding back my vessel

Through turbulent tides
My journey will set sail

If only I did realized
I always was afloat.

Lessons are not learned
In untouched perfection.
Human name of pain
All to lose attention.

Resistance will then breed
When we try to avoid
Listening and learning
Away from all the noise.

But when our eyes will open
Change and redirection
To understand our growth
Through smoke to our reflection.

To make waves
Is a way to speak
Without making noise
And contribute to pollution
For in our depths
The light shines through.

Do we ever fly?
Or are we bound to sink?

For in the sinking
We learn to kick,
We learn to paddle,
We learn to float,
And learn to swim.

In swimming
We see the horizon
And save ourselves.

Had I known
Simplicity as my match
And not my hustle
Would I have changed?
Or just kept going?

My lesson of sincerity
Was a path to take
Holding heavy burden
All to let it go
And to feel the difference.

I will not stand
And shake my fists
My self-serving points
Will shatter souls
The rumbling echoes
Beyond my plight
Who was I serving
Anyway.

There is strength
In my perceived weakness
It shows me lessons
I was ignoring.

To rush and scream
And complain to all
Indulgence was a tyrant.

When nothing worked
And all the fault
Fell on mu handheld mirror.

I slowed it down
to nurture well
my accepted grace within.

LETTING GO

It can be as easy as releasing your grip.

It served a purpose, but now you're holding onto it while it's weighing you down.

When I let go
Is when I swim
And surf
And glide
And skip.
But first, I must
Let go of all
To see the skill within.

If water can flow
And nurture bodies
While carving canyons
And powering homes
From a simple drop
To ocean's deep
So can our flesh
When we believe.

It's time I release
Pain that was attempting
To protect me
And the fear
That raised me.

The cycle is cracked
And I'm ripping it open
To remove the shards
That kept my flesh raw
Wounds will heal
And cycles left behind
While scars strengthen skin
And sands become of you.

Change, my friend
I thought, my foe
The tides massage
My rougher edge.
To stay in place
Would swim in stagnance
When I prefer
To glide on through.

Why seek explanation
Or understanding
When you can accept
And release
For your own comfort?

Fickle friend
I hear you
But I do not need you
For a greater life
I listen
I understand
I do not change you
But leave you there.

A maze with no exit
And ever changing
Feeling every un-kept thorn
And damp wound
Look up
She said
There is no ceiling
Holding you in
There's always a way
When you're ready.

Meant to breathe
Meant for calm
No reason not to
Why do I keep
My soul away
A sabotaged self
With no one for blame
Make the change
Not the complaint.

Am I a victim?
A product of circumstance?
Or ruler of my life?

I put down my weapons
I am not the warrior.

I put down my shields
I am not the defender.

I pick up my crown
I am the power.

I pick up the kingdom's map
I know what is mine.

And I leave *them* to battle
This losing war.

Release your past
And greet your now
To find out who
You always were
All at once
We live it true
Your voice is how
You see it through.

With free thought minds
We can attest
The delight in its unravel.

Un-needing of
Restraints at arms
The safety walls in shambles.

A Trojan horse
We welcomed in
Un-knowing of its grip.

Brighter tides
And softer waves
Now teach of calmer seas.

Learning to walk
Means building muscles
Not a guarantee
To scrape my knees
As a rite of passage.

MINDFULNESS

The moment is always yours for the taking.

I am not certain of anything in my life, other than this exact moment as it's happening.

Oh how we forget
The simple pleasures
Those from in between
With open eyes
And listening ears
Playfully wondering
Without wanting
Because that's all
We'll ever need.

The water's edge
Is right in front
With ebbs and flows
Much like my own
I dream of its constant sound
And wait patiently.

I do not know what tomorrow brings
And I cannot change what yesterday brought.
I surely can participate
In this moment's offering - that is my only certainty.

But if my thoughts are in tomorrow
And yesterday's undoing,
How can I be the master
Of this narrow sate of stillness?

It passes and I lose out.
Tomorrow is now yesterday.
Already 10 years later.

Why do flowers grow?
Why do birds sing?
Why do streams flow
And humans dream?

There is a spark
A heart's pull
That whispers the way
To joy's embrace.

No limbs or cells
But smiles back
To watch us grow
And silently wait.

As the roaring waves
Mould the shore
A million and one stones
Move to the beat
The rhythm builds
For our feet to enjoy.

When I stop
I truly see
The beauty
That surrounds me.

Unveiling the landscape
The fog takes flight
As water droplets
Fill the sky.

The ins and outs
Of my breath
Mirror the water
As my reflection
Smiles back
To greet me.

There's a lightness
Under my feet
It moves my soul
My fingertip buzz
And all is well.

Silent smiles
With ripple's joy
A gift to all
A voice we know.

It's not about
The pursuit
Nor destination
But where your feet
Are firmly planted
When your breath
Catches.

You'll find me
Among the fields
The trees
The oceans
Wanting for nothing
Because in the nothing
I find peace.

DESIRE

It's in the knowing of what we want,
that we can walk towards it.

Ease comes when you stop trying,
and move with purpose instead.

Where will I go?
What will I do?
How will I live?

The unanswered questions
Met with echoes.
It's not in the questioning
But in the desire.

Where do I want to go?
What do I want to do?
How do I want to live?

That answers are found.

It's in the outcome
Of my greatest wants
That I must focus
My attention
Not my greatest fears
Nor my greatest pains
It's in desired outcome
Not unwanted states.

Although our ships are stocked and packed
We may not want to board.
Dragging our feet, we walk it well
Complaining 'til our time to plank.

What if we knew, well and true
That these shackles never locked?
We'd push them off and wave goodbye
As they move to sea and sail on through.

I ask you simply
For what you want
You give me needs
But not desire.

That spark, that light, that joyous glimmer
The one that speaks to souls.

Open your hand
Let go your grip
And tell me now
What serves you well?

Desire is sold
As decadence
A gluttonous endeavour.

When it's our right
Divinely ours
To taste extravagance.

To glide in ease
And feel the buzz,
Better than any vice.

Truth be told
They sold me strength
Which accompanied its reason.

I never needed
Brawn or force
To sit in simple delight.

Why would I walk
When I can run
Even skip and dance?

Your path is safe
But mine is free
With birds singing symphonies.

Let go of status quo
Stagnancy in maintenance.

Remove your blocks
The *can'ts* and *shoulds*

What do you want
Without your lack?

Desire is a visible key
Unlocking untold gold
Reach in your pocket
And hold it up
To walk toward unburied chests.

A falsehood *should*
Taught fairly well
Their fear in our found choice.

It's because they know
They lost control
When we danced with our found voice.

Wishing wells
Will eat your coins
Unless you believe
In reciprocity.

None can help
Until you feel
Joy in freely
Receiving.

Will you gain
With their pride
Or fall in line
Like those before?

Flight is free
And so is thought
When will you see
What you were taught?

How do I want to feel?
Calmness, joyous living, loving care, healthy vitality, and prosperous delight.
While I close my eyes
It's all there
No need of change
Or movement bare
Just open welcome
And willing to feel.

BEING

The stillness of who you are is the poetry of your life.

When did we decide that seeking to be anyone other than ourselves is how we will get ahead in life?

The cost of living without being:
To eat without tasting
To sleep without resting
To achieve without enjoying
To like without loving
To gain without experiencing
Is to exist as flesh
But never as a soul.

With their quiet vows
A place unknown
The trampled dance
And tickled toes
For man's made quest
Of fields of bold
We sit here quietly
And count our gold.

So disconnected from each other
We are souls living in bodies
All searching for the same thing
All screaming for the same thing
But all the while
We always had it
It was all we needed
To turn around
From all our noise
And love ourselves
Unconditionally.

Can I find what I seek?
Can I stop the yearning?
Perhaps the truth lies in the needing.
What is the why?
The answer is not the solution
But in the question.

How did I not see?
How did I not hear?
The confusion no longer serves me,
But the step forward does.

My job is not the how
My job is not the why
It's the piece of me
That prances in streets
Knowing none of it matters
For me to be.

Glowing smiles
And warm greetings
A fleeting glance
With teeth of grin
How far it goes
Recipient knows
For bright horizons
And paths unknown.

We are all
Imperfect
And that's what makes us
Perfect
If only
We knew.

It's not how I imagined it
But is it ever?
With guided sight
I can navigate
But the map is ever changing.

Why do we qualify
And quantify
Our worth
In the hands of another
While singing winds
And dancing trees
Exist in harmony
Without.

To live in delight
With only gain
Love is
Like a warm glow
Rejecting all else
The ease in being
With no chase
No seeking
But allowing
And receiving.

Thank you
To the one who listens
And watches
Thriving in existence
For no gain at all.

The beauty
Of simplicity
Is unmatched
By any accessory
You add.

Here I am
At the beginning
Where it all started
Though a blink
So much between
If you end
At the start
Did you lose
Or gain it all?

Looking to others
To be inspired
All I needed
Was to sit
And hold my pen
Because
It was never about them.

Without suppression
Without rebellion
Your essence shines
And greets you.

If I am not
In alignment
And ease
I will be challenged
Then supported
To find Myself
Again.

Maybe it's in
The knowing
Of where you started
And loving it all the same
That you are truly born.

Getting out of my way,
Who is standing there?

The part of me that fears
The part of me that stays.
I thought I needed to save myself
And block away the pain.

But what I blocked
Was my potential
And the saving I needed
Was from myself.

My greatest threat
Now, my greatest ally
Because if I have potential
So does she
And two forces are greater than one.

She made waves
Not for others
But for herself
Knowing full well
Ripples stir oceans.

Determined fools
Aren't we enough
For flight and destiny?

We will awake
Our wealth namesake
With battles long forgotten.

Known simplicity
Anticipates its peace
Why would I call
Upon its rival
To wear a badge of honour?
The finer things
Come to me sound
And I awake
In dignity.

I will not starve for need
I will wait for fruition.
In the waiting
I learn the skills
As if in training
Preparing to receive.

No longer looking
I am what I seek
Without fault
Definition of love
A journey's seek
Complete.

ABOUT THE AUTHOR

Who is Kiki?
Kiki Carr was born in Ontario, Canada and grew up in a small city East of Toronto. Graduating from Ontario Tech University with a Bachelor of Arts, she immersed herself in studying domestic violence, women's studies, victimology, psychology, and sought to understand why people do what they do. She is currently a student of mindfulness and uses this as a tool for her writing and daily living.

Kiki is a writer and author who hopes for readers to experience a grounding and mindfulness practice as they read her words. She uses her education and personal experiences to show others how she lives a life of delight. In 2019, she was published in her first co-authored book, *Unleashing Her Wild,* a collection of stories written by women who have found a deep connection to intuition and instinct. Her second co-authored book *She's No Longer Silent,* published in 2020, is a collection of stories from women speaking out about trauma, mental illness, and social injustice.

Where can you find Kiki?

Kiki has moved all of her writing and creativity to one platform, rather than across various social media spaces. In a loud online world full of noise and content, she wanted to get quiet and intentional. You can find her in one simple and mindful space: her website at www.kikicarr.com. When you visit her website, you are being invited into her grounded corner of the universe. Here you can find more books, more readings, and more of yourself.

"Writing is expression, reading is an experience."

—Kiki Carr: For all my Wild Readers

Who is a Wild Reader?

A person who loves to immerse themselves in the written word and to reflect inward. A Wild Reader is someone who lives life differently and is able to feel what they read. If you are a Wild Reader and you want to receive more words to reflect and move through, head to www.kikicarr.com to allow your email inbox to experience more offerings. *I hope that you will join me there.*

CPSIA information can be obtained
at www.ICGtesting.com
Printed in the USA
LVHW041017060521
686676LV00007B/795

9 781777 176037